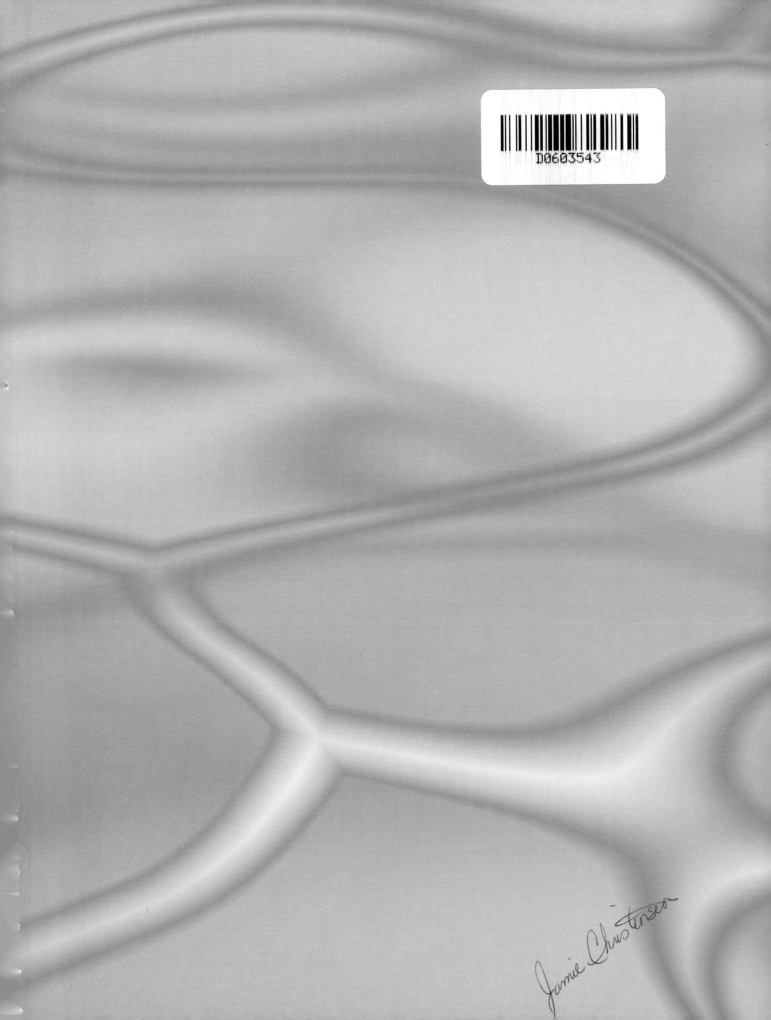

Jamie Christensen

A COMPLETE GUIDE TO DISCOVERING

MEDITATION

PETER HARRISON

Published in 2001 by Caxton Editions
20 Bloomsbury Street
London WC1B 3JH
a member of the Caxton Publishing Group

© 2001 Caxton Publishing Group
Reprint 2002 , 2003
Designed and produced for Caxton Editions
by Open Door Limited
Rutland, United Kingdom

Editing: Mary Morton
Coordination and Typesetting: Jane Booth
Digital Imagery © copyright 2001 PhotoDisc, Inc.

Title: MEDITATION
ISBN: 1-84067-290-0

IMPORTANT NOTICE
This book is not intended to be a substitute for medical advice or
treatment. Any person with a condition requiring medical attention
should consult a qualified medical practitioner or suitable therapist.

A COMPLETE GUIDE TO DISCOVERING

MEDITATION

PETER HARRISON

CAXTON EDITIONS

CONTENTS

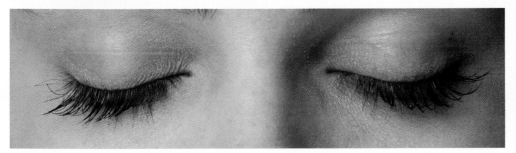

ON BEING AND BECOMING

What is meditation, and, since there are already over a thousand books in print on the subject and over one million references to it on the world wide web, why another book?

Clearly there are many methods and approaches to meditation, but these are, after all, methods and approaches. Meditation is the objective. What is it, how can we discover or realise it, and how do we recognise it when we have achieved it?

It would be foolish to try to define meditation — it is beyond definition and words will surely fail us. It can be realised and recognised only in our immediate awareness of its reality. All methods and approaches which can be used in the practice of meditation are valid only in so far as they bring us to this immediate awareness, only in so far as they can lead us to the threshold of meditation — and the door is always open.

To open up the field of our enquiry it may be useful to consider the following incident which occurred to a young lady, well practised in meditation. She related that she was cleaning her house, like Martha in the gospels busily engaged in many things, pre-occupied with a busy schedule. She entered the room in which she thought her three-month-old baby was sleeping, and was suddenly brought to her senses. She recalled the baby was wide awake and the room was filled with a peaceful, blissful and silent presence. This made a startling contrast to her own state, which she saw to be an unnecessarily noisy turmoil. She quickly left the room to "compose" herself. The baby, she was convinced, was in meditation.

Every detail of this lady's observation carried the authenticity of clear and direct perception and we can draw from it many pointers to our basic questions concerning meditation.

MEDITATION IS WHAT YOU ARE – NOT WHAT YOU DO

Right: which of us has not been aware of qualities of meditation in ourselves in the presence of a new-born child?

It seems important to establish this from the beginning. We have already acknowledged that there are many methods and approaches to meditation. Some will be outlined in this book. However, this baby was not "practising" anything – it was simply enjoying its Being. There seems to be an almost universal recognition of this – which of us has not been aware of qualities of meditation in ourselves in the presence of a new-born child?

MEDITATION IS FOR EVERYBODY

There is no reason to believe that this baby was any different to any other. The very qualities of uninhibited, spacious joyfulness that we would commonly attribute to meditation is what also attracts people in the new-born babe. Hence the insistence, in all traditions, on being "born again", returning to the state of childlike innocence. Throughout this book we will return to this theme again and again. Meditation, or meditative awareness, is our inherent, natural birthright. It is the fullness of awareness which illuminates our essential, timeless Being.

Furthermore, although, like Esau the Hairy Hunter, we sell this precious birthright for a "mess of pottage", in truth, it never goes away from us. To coin a phrase, "in meditative awareness we live and move and have our being" whether we are aware of it or not. From this arises our longing for peace, for space in our lives, for freedom from stress, limitation and isolation and eventually the search for all these things through the practice of meditation in some form or other.

Below: the very qualities of uninhibited, spacious joyfulness that we would commonly attribute to meditation is what also attracts people in the new-born babe.

MEDITATION IS BEYOND RELIGIOUS FORM

All of the great religious traditions have within them an approach to meditation. For the beginner to approach meditation through the forms and symbols of a familiar religious culture makes obvious sense. However, it should be equally obvious that, because of the very nature of belief, there may be difficulty in going beyond the form to the direct experience of unconditioned meditative awareness. In some cases specific aims or goals connected to these religious forms are set up and these can be impenetrable barriers to true experience of meditation. Again the difference is between the direct and unitive experience of Being and the formal practice based on a system of belief. Since none of us were born religious, this being something taught later within the family, culture and tradition into which we are born, it follows that the meditative awareness which is inherent at birth is not subject to or dependent on any particular religious form or practice, helpful though these may be in providing us with the structures to recognise and maintain it.

MEDITATION REFLECTS

Only in meditative awareness do we clearly see the ever-changing circumstances of our lives. Without this clarity our perceptions are clouded by preconceptions, misconceptions and prejudices, ideas, opinions and beliefs. From time to time we are honest enough to recognise and admit this in ourselves – then we may seek a remedy and the remedy will ultimately be meditation.

Far left: all of the great religious traditions have within them an approach to meditation. For the beginner to approach meditation through the forms and symbols of a familiar religious culture makes obvious sense.

Below: in the observation given by the mother with her meditative baby the lady was able clearly to recognise and acknowledge the meditative awareness with which the room was filled.

In the observation given by the mother with her meditative baby the lady was able clearly to recognise and acknowledge the meditative awareness with which the room was filled. This same awareness illuminated her own inner chaos. She realised on reflection that at this moment she had made the wrong choice – she fled the room with its atmosphere of meditative awareness in order to re-arrange the chaos. As if there were a choice between one or the other when the evident truth was that both could exist together.

The baby meanwhile continued to exercise its limbs as babies do – in random movements which eventually result in a more or less harmonious co-ordination of the physical body with the energies flowing through it and the mind directing the movements. The baby continued to gurgle and practise sounds which would eventually translate into the ability to communicate through speech, none of which in any way disturbed the meditative awareness.

The difference between this meditative awareness and the practice of meditation, between our essential, unchanging being and the ever-changing circumstances of our lives, can be illustrated by a number or analogies which will now be outlined.

SOME ANALOGIES

In London's Greenwich Park, close to the Observatory, there is a white line drawn on the ground indicating the meridian. We can easily stand with one foot in the eastern and one foot in the western hemisphere. The art of meditative awareness is to stand with one foot in both the situations outlined earlier. Paradoxically it is possible to be fully established in stillness and at the same time fully involved in action. This may sound impossible, but meditation knows it to be so through direct experience. The list below is not exhaustive, but a consideration of the above, with some practical experiments, may help us to understand and appreciate meditation

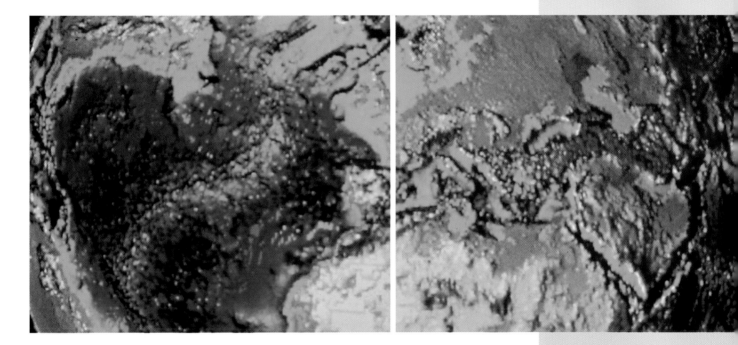

BEING	BECOMING
Christ	Jesus
Silence	Sound
Stillness	Movement
Clear light	Colours
The silver screen	Moving pictures
Timeless eternity	Past and future

Above: in London's Greenwich Park, close to the Observatory, there is a white line drawn on the ground indicating the meridian. We can easily stand with one foot in the eastern and one foot in the western hemisphere.

In the west the predominant religion of Christianity shows Jesus as the person who knew within himself or realised the Universal Being, thus being fully man and fully God. St Paul states that we have all "sinned and so fall short of the glory of God". To sin means to miss the mark; to lose the living connection to our essential source; to lose meditative awareness and become totally involved in our personal and petty limitations so that our lives become "a tale told by an idiot (meaning private person in Greek) full of sound and fury, signifying nothing".

It may be useful here to consider a series of paintings by Hieronymus Bosch, a painter whose every brushstroke indicates meditative awareness and who, significantly, often inserts his self-portrait into the midst of the apparent chaos of his imagery, witnessing the scene from within with a detached compassion.

In *Christ Mocked* (National Gallery, London) Bosch shows the figure of Jesus surrounded by four types of humanity – the priest/pedant, the warrior, the merchant and the peasant labourer (a remarkable parallel to the four broad castes of the Indian system). Each looks directly at him, each has direct contact, each is antagonistic.

In *Ecce Homo* (Escorial, Madrid) the same four types are in evidence, more grossly caricatured, but they are no longer in direct contact, no longer in touch – even their gaze is no longer direct. We are approaching what Shakespeare so masterfully describes as: "Man, proud man, most ignorant of that his most assured – his glassy essence."

Left: in the west the predominant religion of Christianity shows Jesus as the person who knew within himself or realised the Universal Being, thus being fully man and fully God.

Below: a Christian statue of Jesus.

Finally, in the magnificent *Ascent to Calvary* (Ghent) the figure of Jesus is placed right in the centre of the picture. Substantial and earthy yet very still and conveying meditative awareness, he is surrounded by a surging sea of caricatures of every type of human folly and ignorance all apparently oblivious of the silent presence in their midst. Even Saint Veronica is shown simpering devoutly at the image of Jesus imprinted on her handkerchief in complete ignorance of the living presence of Christ right beside her. (Imagine what courage it required to paint this in the times of religious sensitivity and intolerance through which Bosch lived.)

Reflection on this series of three pictures seems to indicate how we lose our "birthright" of peaceful, joyful, meditative awareness – hence the need for meditation and the growing interest in meditation as the pace of life quickens.

Sound and Silence

Now let us turn our attention to the analogy of sound and silence. First, a poem for your delight:

Earth Chant

Listen, can you hear it?
Can you hear the silence?
And beyond the silence –
Earth sings, and the song is creation.
In deepest silence, deep depth of being,
In the womb of creation,
heart throb of loving,
The impulse of living, harmonious
life-song,
Rises out of the silence,
to manifest being:
Listen, can you hear it?
Earth song – Earth sings –
And the song is creation.
Singing praise to the Lord that gave
life to the being,
Praise to the glory of mountain
and meadow,
Sings in the veins of the rivers,
the breath of the forest,
In the roar of the ocean,
the rhythm of raindrops,
Harmonious the song,
cosmic the chorus.
Listen, can you hear it?
Chant of the cosmos,
Chorus of love,
Returning to silence,
Deep depth of being,
Where all sound returns
Returning to silence, returning to
peace.

Ours now to join in the
chant of creation,
The song in the cavern –
Deepest depth of our being,
Wellspring of lovesurge
From the throne of the silence.
Sound out the tocsin of regeneration,
Resonating through earth ways
The rhymes of formation,
Through energies pathways,
The pulsebeats of living,
Sings in the breath,
Fulfilling and cleansing,
Warmed by the sun,
Bright be your vision,
Warmth to your heart,
Joy to the earth,
This joyful creation.

Earth sings earth's song
And the song is creation,
Returning to silence –
returning to peace
Returning... returning –
Listen – can you hear it?

Returning forever to silence and peace.

Listening is one of the great keys to awareness. It connects directly to sound and the natural medium for sound is space and the essential quality of space is joy. Here is a simple exercise in listening awareness.

Sit comfortably and at ease with your back erect without strain, and if possible let the spine be self-supporting. Focus your awareness at the point where the bridge of the nose meets the upper lip and experience the sense of touch. You will be able to feel the breath entering hands and face. Feel the weight of your body, keep in touch.

Now begin to listen – not to anything in particular, but just listen to all the sounds that come to your awareness. Avoid naming the sounds, talking to yourself about them, liking or disliking them – just listen. As your listening extends, be in touch with the expansion of space in your awareness. Hear all the sounds and acknowledge their harmony with each other. As you listen, acknowledge also the silence. Observe how all the sounds that

Below: listening is one of the great keys to awareness.

and leaving the nostrils. Do not try to change anything; simply feel the moving air entering and leaving the nostrils. Be in touch. Now extend your awareness to include the entire energy field of the body – from the crown of the head to the tips of your toes. Feel the air playing on your bare skin, your come to your awareness arise out of silence, how they resonate through and are sustained by the silence and how they dissolve back into the silence. Hear both the silence and the sounds and remain in the awareness of space.

Far left: listening connects directly to sound and the natural medium for sound is space and the essential quality of space is joy.

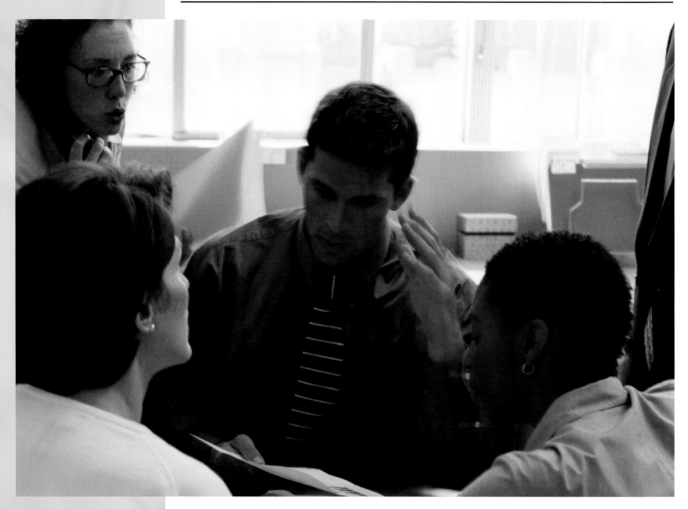

Above: listening awareness can be tried even in conversation. When others are speaking, listen only to the sound of their voices – do not focus on the words.

You may have noticed in this practice the clear distinction between the changing sounds, constantly rising and falling, and the never-changing, unmoving silence. With practice comes the ability to stand quite comfortably with one foot in the silence and one foot in the sound – fully present in both. The art is in not naming the sounds. You may have the courage to try this out, even in conversation. When others are speaking, listen only to the sound of their voices – do not focus on the words. You may be amazed by what you hear in this new approach to communication. When speaking yourself, listen only to the sound of your own voice as it speaks. After all – if you are not prepared to listen to your own speech, why would anyone else be expected to listen to it? This, too, brings in a new dimension to communication. Too often the person speaking is at the same time preparing the next sentence whilst the person listening is, in fact, busily rehearsing their response – and both end up wondering why there is no communication or understanding.

A women came to a meditation teacher. She was almost a nervous wreck – tense, worried and very haggard. Her problem was lack of proper sleep. For too long she had been plagued by her husband's snoring. Night after night he snored away. Night after night she had struggled to get to sleep, to no avail. Ear plugs she had tried, but they were no use. Still the snoring was ringing in her ears. Sedatives had had no effect against this mighty snoring. Now she was desperate, almost mad. What could she do?

The teacher asked, "Have you tried listening to the snoring?"
"What! Are you mad?", cried the poor woman. "I don't want to hear it. That's what's keeping me awake. I can't stand it and you want me to listen to it?"

Patiently the teacher taught her about silence and how not to name, like or dislike the sound, but how to really listen to it.

One week later she came back – dancing – looking 20 years younger. "I thought that you were crazy, but you were right", she cried. "I tried it the way you showed me. What could I lose? I'd tried everything else. And it worked. It was such a beautiful lullaby – it sent me straight to sleep. "

And so we can meditate in both sound and silence.

Below: listening awareness can even help the frustrated partners of snorers achieve a good night's sleep.

STILLNESS AND MOVEMENT

"What is action, what is inaction?" asks the *Bhagavad Geeta*, admitting that even the wise are baffled. As if that were not enough to confuse us who thought it was a pretty straight-forward matter, it then goes on to discuss action in inaction and inaction in action! To make matters even worse we are eventually informed that for the truly wise there is the clear understanding that, in the midst of every type of activity, "I do nothing at all".

Far left: even when we collapse exhausted into our beds at night we are not allowed to rest. Perhaps not surprisingly, the mind continues in active mode – churning out dreams.

Below: more than ever, most of us are driven by action. Even our so-called leisure time and recreational activities reflect this.

Now, possibly more than ever, most of us are driven by action. Even our so-called leisure time and recreational activities reflect this. Faster, louder music, fast cars in the fast lane – we even have fast food, most of which is so indigestible that it is anything but. Instant this and instant that – the list is endless. Even when we collapse exhausted into our beds at night we are not allowed to rest. Perhaps not surprisingly, the mind continues in active mode – churning out dreams.

Some branches of the health industry, particularly psychiatrists, perhaps because of their own vested interests, reassure us that this is not only OK, but in fact necessary to our health. To add further insult to injury they then promulgate the "scientific fact" that we need eight hours' sleep per night, thus suggesting that we spend one-third of our precious lifetime in oblivion!

Let us fall still a moment and think. Consider the turnover of the health industry in terms of sedatives and sleeping pills and, of course, the increasingly necessary pick-me-up pills. More usefully, consider the following scenario – there will be few of us who haven't had this experience. You wake up bright as a button, refreshed and full of energy only to find it is still "too early" – let's say five o'clock in the morning. It's still dark out there and probably cold. Furthermore, it's so warm and comfy in bed, you roll over and go back for a bit more sleep – after all, you deserve it and there is another busy day ahead.

How did you feel next time you woke up? Was there the same bright, vibrant energy flowing, the same clarity of mind? The same joie de vivre? If not, it is because the fresh energy made available in deep sleep – where there are no desires or dreams – has largely been dissipated by the restless mind. Perhaps, after all the *Bhagavad Geeta* is right, and not only is this question of activity and movement in contrast to deep rest and stillness worth considering, but also the quality of our lives is profoundly influenced by our practical understanding of these apparently irreconcilable opposites.

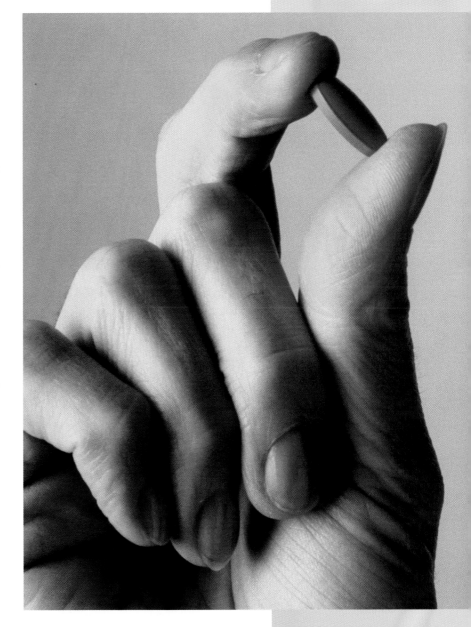

Below: consider the turnover of the health industry in terms of sedatives and sleeping pills and, of course, the increasingly necessary pick-me-up pills.

Above: meditation leads us to realise that deep within each one of us is a vast ocean of stillness and silence.

Meditation reveals that, just as sound rests in the silence from which it arises, all movement is based on the stillness from which it arises. Meditation leads us to realise that deep within each one of us is a vast ocean of stillness and silence. Meditative awareness allows us to enter activity and yet remain connected to that silence. In full awareness, paradoxically, we are fully involved in the movement and at the same time totally detached in the stillness. How can we approach this? Why is it so important?

Consider a universal activity common to us all. Eating. In all traditional societies of every religious persuasion, it was common practice before eating to gather together in silence – to say grace in some form or another – and to fall still from all variety of activities . What a difference this makes to the unity of families and the community of friends! (In silence and stillness is our true common unity which may then be expressed in all our relationships.)

Above: in all traditional societies it was common practice before eating to gather together in silence – to say grace.

SOME ANALOGIES

We are now in a position to "bless" the food we are about to eat with our intelligent consideration. Not a bad idea in view of the fact that it is now generally understood that what we eat has a profound effect on our bodies, minds, emotions and our general well-being. We now proceed to taste the food we eat, a simple activity so profoundly linked to our enjoyment of life and the digestive process that will also guide us to measure and regulate our intake so we do not overburden ourselves with too much of the wrong thing. And when we have had sufficient we can return to silence and stillness to mark the end of the activity before going about our next business.

This points the way to a practical approach which will enable us to master the meditative art of "action in inaction and inaction in action". It can be extended throughout the day in such a way that every new activity can be preceded by a return to stillness and ended in the same way.

Below: what we eat has a profound effect on our bodies.

RETURNING TO STILLNESS

Our days are filled with activity. Unwittingly we rush from one activity to another without pausing to "take stock". This not only results in a very unmeasured use of energy (observe the effort we put into closing a car door, for example), but it also sets in motion a kind of flywheel effect which gathers increasing momentum throughout the day, leaving us exhausted and stressed in the evening and unable to relax. The remedy to this state of affairs is to acknowledge that the day is, in fact, made up of a series of individual activities, each of which requires our due care and attention. To enable this to be given to each activity – as in the example of eating discussed above – it makes sense to start each activity from a position of stillness and silent awareness; to maintain this awareness throughout the activity to the best of our ability; and to finalise the activity with a return to rest before moving on. In the same way that sleep at night refreshes us and recharges our energy, such a practice followed throughout the day will reduce stress and exhaustion and maintain our levels of alertness and enthusiasm. We would be well on the way to meditation in action.

Above: Our days are filled with activity. Unwittingly we rush from one activity to another without pausing to "take stock".

Below: to give an example of this returning to stillness, consider another activity most will be familiar with – driving a car.

To give an example of this returning to stillness, consider another activity most will be familiar with – driving a car. Before starting the car, relax in the seat. Focus your awareness on the moving air entering and leaving the nostrils at the point where the bridge of the nose meets the upper lip. Simply observe the flow of breath at this point for a short while. This has the effect of putting us in touch. Now acknowledge the entire energy field of your body from the crown of the head to the toes. Acknowledge the weight of your body on the car seat and the play of air on your face and hands. Be in touch with yourself. Now let your hearing extend into the space all around you, just hearing the sounds without naming them or liking and disliking them.

Return to your centre, your still point, and from this point of enhanced awareness and alertness start the engine and proceed safely on your way. At the end of the journey, during which you will no doubt have been less inclined to impatience, more relaxed and polite to your fellow road-users, as you turn off the ignition and the engine stops running, return yourself to your natural stillness and leave behind all the motion and noise of the journey before moving on to the next activity. .

In this way we can measure out our days by the natural rhythm of movement and rest and, with practice, the stillness and silence of meditative awareness will pervade even our most strenuous exertions.

Clear Light and the Spectrum

Over three hundred years ago Isaac Newton demonstrated this magical fact of our everyday existence, which is still as fresh, startling and awe-inspiring today as it must have been to his original audience. He created a dark room with a screen. In one of the blinds he made a small, neat hole which allowed a ray of sunlight to pass onto the screen. Then he placed a prism (a piece of cut glass with at least three sides) between the pinhole and the screen. The clear light of the sunbeam separated into bands of light, each displaying a different colour – red, orange yellow, green, blue,

indigo and violet – the colours of the rainbow. This we call the spectrum, a word which means simply spectacle or appearance. Most of us will have been intrigued by a similar demonstration in the science laboratory in school. Since colour defines form, it follows that all the objects of our awareness arise in a similar way. This brings us on quite naturally to another analogy which is often used to indicate the nature of meditative awareness and the difference between being and becoming.

Above: most of us will have been intrigued by a demonstration such as that performed by Newton when he revealed the colour spectrum to his audience. Since colour defines form, it follows that all the objects of our awareness arise in a similar way.

The Silver Screen and the Movies

As we are all aware, in the cinema a powerful white light is directed by a projector onto a silver screen. A reel of film is passed at rapid speed between the screen and the projector, creating an extremely lifelike series of images for our entertainment. We enjoy the film.

Since the reel of film is made up of a series of "still frames", each separated by a row of perforations for editing purposes, and since furthermore there is a fast-revolving, bladed fan necessary for the cooling of the intense heat generated by the bulb of the projector, we are, in fact, a lot of the time gazing at an empty screen. This is more apparent in watching the early films where the speed of projection was so slow that the movements depicted on the screen are jerky rather than smooth-flowing. So efficient is modern technology that it has long been possible to flash messages on the screen which appear and disappear so rapidly that the eye does not register them yet they are still observed on the screen of our awareness and may influence our behaviour. Hence the strict restrictive regulations on any form of "subliminal messaging".

On the silver screen we may see stories of love and hate, war and peace, tragedy and comedy – the whole spectrum of human experience, realistically presented. We may allow ourselves to become completely involved in the plot, identify with the characters, be frightened out of our lives or convulsed with laughter. The whole range of human emotions can be triggered by the magical illusion of the cinema, which must account for its enduring popularity.

When the movie is over and the projector is turned off the silver screen is revealed just as it was before all the sound and fury, completely untouched by the events depicted on its surface.

Analogies are never 100 per cent precise, but this one comes close to it. If we can imagine that the silver screen represents the screen of our conscious awareness, the projected images flickering on the screen would be the events of our daily life inviting our response. We may, in meditative awareness, remain with the unchanging screen, while at the same time fully participating in the play of creation, enjoying it for what it is but remaining free of its involvements. This, again, would be meditation in action.

ETERNITY AND PASSING TIME

Time is yet another magical mystery in our lives. Generally we all live by the clock and this is functional and necessary for arriving at work on time, keeping appointments and the necessities of communication in everyday life. The danger is that we gradually become time-bound, and this can create difficulties. Although we all reasonably and harmoniously agree on clock-time and its usefulness, we all appreciate that time is a very subjective phenomenon. We have all experienced occasions where time has literally "flown by", usually when we are really enjoying ourselves, and occasions when time has dragged by interminably, even occasions when time has "stood still".

In all cultures and traditions there is an almost universal agreement to divide time three ways – the past, the present and the future. At one level this is functional and convenient. But consider. The past exists only in our memory and our memory is only present to us in our present awareness, in other words NOW. The future is non-existent, something we project on the basis of our past experience according to our dreams and desires. And the much-vaunted "present moment" cannot be grasped – even before it is properly perceived, it has raced into the past!
We may practise meditation in time, a thousand repetitions of this mantra

(time and counting go hand in hand), for instance. We may "sit" in meditation for half an hour or so until the incense stick burns down, or use any number of other devices, but ultimately who is counting? Being time-bound and subject to calculation such activities are also result-orientated and, as such, will be a barrier to the full experience of meditative awareness.

Fall still using the method suggested previously. When connected to the breath and the energy field of your body, follow the next inhalation with your full awareness and observe the point where it naturally changes to exhalation. Rest awareness at this point. Consider the question "How old am I?", without any urgency to acquire an answer. Avoid all the answers that the mind can come up with – sooner or later you will enter your own timeless presence.

Far left: generally we all live by the clock and this is functional and necessary for arriving at work on time, keeping appointments and the necessities of communication in everyday life.

In the *Katha Upanishad* it is stated that "Self rides on the chariot of the body". We may make an analogy in more modern terms. Suppose you are travelling in a fast-moving, modern train. These are often capable of speeds of well over a hundred miles per hour. Your view through the window is limited and the passing scenery, at least that closest to you, is passing rapidly in a confusing blur. So it is when we are identified with the body. Events seem to impose themselves on us. We even use the word "emergency" to indicate a crisis situation, but every event that occurs in our awareness emerges from the silent-still presence and returns into it. Now consider if, instead of being inside the train, getting a one-sided view of your situation as it flashes by you, you were viewing the progress of the train from a helicopter tracking it from some height.

Now you would be able to see quite clearly where the train has come from – clear hindsight. You would be able to observe where it was, at any given moment and, more crucially, you would be able to observe quite clearly the track ahead. With adequate communication links to the train you would be able to warn of dangers before they turned into disasters (prudent foresight) and all this would take place with the awareness of the pilot. So "Awakened intelligence, the sure-footed charioteer" as the *Katha Upanishad* puts it.

The *Bhagavad Geeta* states: "That which is (Being) shall never cease to be; that which is not shall never be. Both these are self-evident to the knower of the essence." Hence the importance of the dualities outlined in this exploration of analogies.

Like the person in Greenwich bestriding the meridian line, with one foot in the east and one in the west, the person who knows meditation can be fully and wholeheartedly engaged in the activities of life, enjoying life to the full, whilst remaining totally detached and centred in the unchanging Being.

Let us begin with a simple experiment which will make self-evident certain things which are common to the experience of everybody.

Sit comfortably in an upright, self-supporting position. Bring the body to rest and, by attending to the breath, be sure that you are in touch with your energy field. As before, bring your mind to rest by simply listening to the sounds going on all around you without naming them or reacting. Just observe how they arise from silence, resonate through the silence and dissolve back into it. Relax into the space which is becoming more apparent. With patience and your intelligent interest, this practice will begin to free the mind from the burden of its running commentary. Now close your eyes and repeat a simple sentence in your mind. Say to yourself:

*BE STILL AND
KNOW THAT I AM*

Listen – don't think about it – just hear it. Try that again.

Below: in the first part of the experiment our attention was turned out to listen to "external" sounds such as music, conversation or trafic noise. We used our sense of hearing to connect with sound.

This simple experiment shows us a great deal about the nature of our common experience. In the first part of the experiment our attention was turned out to listen to "external" sounds. We used our sense of hearing to connect with sound. In meditative awareness both ears would be fully open and turned outwards. The background of space and silence would be self-evident, acknowledged and appreciated. In non-meditative or unreflective awareness we find half

our hearing is turned inwards to a re-active running commentary on what we are hearing. Reason tells us that this cannot be a satisfying state of affairs and direct experience confirms it.

In the second part of our experiment the attention was turned completely inwards to listen to "internal" sounds. We used our sense of hearing to connect with inner or "subtle" sound.

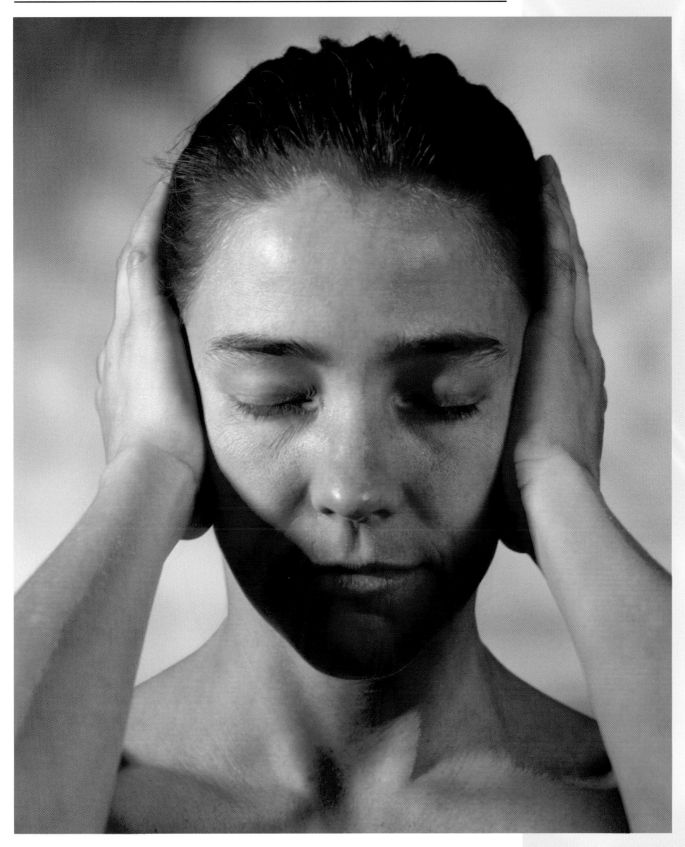

Above: the first important fact to emerge from this simple experiment. The senses can quite easily be turned inwards or outwards to connect with their respective objects.

This is the first important fact to emerge from this simple experiment. The senses can quite easily be turned inwards or outwards to connect with their respective objects. Both modes of experience are extremely useful and there is a time and place for both.

Now consider further. When repeating to yourself "Be still and know that I am", the experience contained four quite distinct aspects:

the action of self-expression – speech;
the perception of self-expression – hearing;
the means of self-expression – sound;
the medium of self-expression – space.

You will have been aware of all these four things simultaneously. If in any doubt, repeat the experiment and take note.

Here is another universal in human experience. Every experience shares these four factors – medium, means, action and perception, all four of which are different aspects of the same energy.

Just as we have five senses, there are five of these fourfold modes of self-expression through which we may come to self-awareness. This is why meditation can be approached through many and various practices involving every sense. It can be understood that everything in our experience is a combination of these five media. Each of us, for example, inhabits a physical body, material and substantial. This is enlivened by a body of energy which carries feeling throughout, from the crown of the head to the tips of the toes. This is informed by our "body of mind" which, if we are mindful, brings intelligent direction to the expression of our feelings. All this is in accordance with our taste, according to our attitude and intentions arising from our "body of individual experience". All this takes place within our body of space, which we become more aware of as meditative awareness deepens.

Before going further into this and examining its practical applications for meditation, here is an example from nature which may help to clarify the co-operation of these fivefold media of self-expression.

Take a seed of grain, itself a form of earth, sown in the soil in due season. Buried in the earth, it receives water from the clouds and fire from the sun, as Chaucer so memorably puts it "from which virtue engendered is the floure". The energy from the seed is thus released allowing it to grow, expand in space and bring forth fruit a hundredfold.

This, harvested and milled, now takes the form of flour for making bread. Each grain of flour, itself a form of earth, contains all that has gone into its generation. When placed in a mixing bowl with the right amount of water, a myriad of such grains of flour coalesce into one malleable substance which we call dough. This, kneaded by loving hands, is informed with energy and air and then put to the fire of the oven for baking, during which it "rises" and in the process becomes full of space. We now have a loaf or rolls of bread – itself a form of earth – "the staff of life", a potent symbol for the body of things.

The mouth-watering smell of fresh-baked bread quickly engenders the desire to eat. Here the substantial food is met in the mouth by saliva and, through mastication, is reduced to a fluid form ready to swallow (gulping down large lumps does not help digestion). In the stomach this is met by the powerful agents of digestion which release the energies in the bread for circulation throughout the body – thus providing substance (flesh) lubrication and vitality in all its forms for the body of the human being.

This example, I hope, illustrates the harmony of interaction of the five elements or media for self-expression in both the environment and the individual. Meditation leads us to this understanding of the basic unity of creation, and meditative awareness enables us to connect with it and maintain that connection in all our daily activities.

An example of this is available through speech – again this is common to everybody, irrespective of variations such as gender, race, colour or religion.

S peech is our prime means of expression. "In the beginning was the Word" is common to alll traditions. Even the movements of our limbs, directed by impulses from the brain through our nervous system, constitute a form of speech.

Speech is an activity utilising space and sound. We connect to it by listening.

Jesus Christ, who was a master scientist of meditative awareness, told his disciples: "Take heed what ye hear: with what measure ye mete, it shall be measured to you" (Mark 4. 24). In listening, we can observe all the measures and qualities mentioned above. Since we spend so much of our time in conversation, either internally or in company, here is an ideal medium through which to bring meditation into action.

These simple principles are very far-reaching, and the good sense of their application should be self-evident.

Above: speech is an activity utilising space and sound. We connect to it by listening.

Below: clearly when speaking we should be connected to the sound of our own voice. After all, if we are not prepared to listen to ourselves, why should we expect anyone else to?

The first relates to space and sound. Clearly when speaking we should be connected to the sound of our own voice. After all, if we are not prepared to listen to ourselves, why should we expect anyone else to? This simple practice alone will begin to transform the way we speak. In fact, every sound we make vibrates throughout our entire energy system and reverberates all around us, affecting both the atmosphere and those in our vicinity. Careful listening increases our sensitivity to these sound vibrations of our own making and gradually our communications become more harmonious.

When others are speaking, we should be listening, too, not busily preparing our responses, straining to get the next word in. If we could listen to the sound of the other person's voice, rather than grasping at the words, a whole new world of meaning would open up for us.

A rabbi was arguing with one of his congregation for many hours. Finally he said, "You are right, I am wrong and I should apologise". Simple enough. Now play with this sentence, experimenting with different emphasis and pitch. This exercise quickly reveals that it is not the bare words that contain the meaning of the speaker. The meaning and intention are in the sound. Listening connects us to increasingly subtle levels of meaning until ultimately we may come to understand that "every word doth almost tell my name, stating its birth, from whence it does proceed" (Shakespeare *Sonnets*).

Being in touch with the sounds connects us with space, which gives us the clarity to move on to the next "measure" we can observe in speech. All sound is vibration of energy, and we can also connect to our own energy through our speech. In fact, the sounds we make and the speech patterns that we employ have a profound effect on our energy field for good or ill. Hence the power and widespread advocation of mantra meditation, the universal love of music and the warnings against the use of blasphemy and violent or abusive language common to all traditions. We all respond to the difference between a dull, lifeless, droning voice and a voice that is enthusiastic, inspiring, filled with life and vitality. To be in touch with the breath and energy that magically gives expression to our

thoughts and feelings is to cultivate the latter. Here is the key to confidence in speech.

Above: even the movements of our limbs, directed by impulses from the brain through our nervous system, constitute a form of speech.

Right: the third measure in speech has to do with fire. The qualities of fire are brightness, clarity and beauty.

Below: the fourth measure is in the realm of water and taste.

The third measure in speech has to do with "fire". The qualities of fire are brightness, clarity and beauty. All these contribute to good communication but nothing more so than the natural intelligence that is inherent in the human voice. We have all marvelled at these qualities, at some times, in other people's voices. Why be reluctant to recognise them and acknowledge them in our own?

The fourth measure is in the realm of water and taste. Not surprisingly the Hindu goddess of speech and learning is called Saraswati – which literally means "the Flowing One". She has three attendants, or handmaidens. Mahi, "the great", because speech flows and shines in space, which is vast, and because speech expands that which is secret within us and brings it into communicative manifestation. Bharati carries and supports our meaning so that it may be available to others whilst Ila signifies praise. Our speech expresses our worth and what we worship or give value to. Its very basis is love, and loving kindness (or the lack of it) is very evident in the sound of the voice.

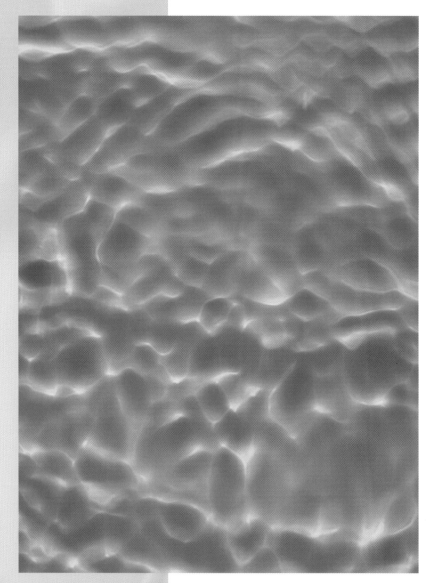

The physical sound of the voice is the fifth measure which brings all the others to our awareness. If we fully connect to the sounds in speech, all this may become apparent, as may the ever-present silence which upholds all sound.

It will be clear from the above that meditative awareness is not helped by negativity and particularly self-degradation in speech — by means of which we literally pass sentence on ourselves. Yet it seems quite common for people to experience a continual flow of negativity and self-criticism in their minds and find this an impenetrable barrier to the practice and experience of meditation. The exercise suggested earlier, on sound and silence, is a powerful antidote to this negativity as well as being the ideal starting place for the examination of the points outlined in this chapter on speech.

GOOD PERSON – GOOD SOCIETY

I have heard that in some Buddhist temples there is a gong placed just inside the entrance. All who enter to practise meditation strike the gong as they go in. At first, this may seem inconsiderate. After all, there you are sitting silently trying to meditate and people keep banging on the gong! How disturbing. But there is method in this madness. The reverberations of the gong recede deeper and deeper into the silence, thus providing an excellent medium for the practice. Here, again, is a demonstration of our principles of sound and silence.

MEDITATION THROUGH BREATH

*Below: breath
awareness is
essential to any
form of
meditation.*

Too often we take our breath for granted. It is clearly connected to our very life force and vitality. Our emotions and our state of mind are also intimately connected to the breath. In the *Ayur Veda*, the science of life, it is clearly stated that the sense of touch pervades all the other senses. Without it, they cannot function. This sense of touch is a function of the life force and vitality, the principal source of which is carried in the breath. Breath awareness is essential to any form of meditation. In the Buddhist tradition a whole science of breathing meditation has been developed in the schools of Vipasanna whilst the entire field of Kundalini yoga, with its emphasis on the chakras or centres of energy transformation, has arisen through attention to the basic function of breath.

For the planet Earth, the sun is the source of vitality and energy. That this affects us is evident. The medical profession has identified and acknowledged "seasonal affective disorder", which basically describes the condition arising if we are deprived of sunlight for lengthy periods of time.

The nourishing qualities of food for all creatures are also clearly derived from the sun. In Sanskrit the word for herbs and plants indicates a form in which light and energy are supported.

Above: for the planet Earth, the sun is the source of vitality and energy. That this affects us is evident.

Below: breath is the principal carrier or vehicle of our life force, or vitality in the body. On entering the body it divides into five streams or functions.

Breath is the principal carrier or vehicle of our life force, or vitality in the body. On entering the body it divides into five streams or functions. This is symbolised in the Celtic cross, which, significantly, is carried at the head of the procession in the Easter celebrations of Christianity.

Apart from revitalising and nourishing the body on inhalation and relaxing and cleansing the body of all toxins through exhalation, it circulates the vital force throughout the body, literally from the crown of the head down to the tips of the toes, ensuring life is everywhere. The breath also fans the fires of digestion. The fifth "stream" of breath connects to our vital intelligence – it being a matter of common experience that what we are thinking and feeling both affects and is affected by our breathing patterns.

All this we can find out for ourselves by being in touch with our breath. Being in touch with our breath opens up the possibility of meditation and meditative awareness. The following practice, if followed, will go some way to re-establishing the natural breathing functions. You may like to record this onto a cassette and use it as a guide until the systematic flow of the practice comes naturally to you.

The key area is the place where the bridge of the nose meets the upper lip. Focus your awareness at this point and be in touch with the moving air as it enters and leaves the nostrils. This is substantial and tangible – you can feel it. If not, persevere until you can. This is a practice to bring deep relaxation to the body and the mind, based on the breathing system and the subtle energy systems which carry the life force throughout the body. You will find that the mind rests very naturally at this point where the bridge of the nose meets the upper lip, and the breath itself is a most natural focus for the mind's attention.

Above: the key area is the place where the bridge of the nose meets the upper lip.

Remember that breath is life, so as you focus at this point where the breath goes in and out of the nostrils, feel that you are in touch with the flow of the life force and all its movements within the body. By focusing at this point of tangible contact with the breath, you will form a centre of awareness of touch and feeling. With no effort on your part, this centre will naturally expand to bring you in touch with the entire energy field of your body, from the crown of your head to the tips of your toes.

Relax into your energised body. Accept what you find there. Do not try to change anything. Simply observe the rise and fall of the breath. As you inhale, observe how your energy field is filled with life, light and energy. As inhalation turns to exhalation, let go of everything you no longer need. Experience the twin functions of breathing – fulfilling and enlivening on the inhalation, relaxing and cleansing on the exhalation.

Remove all effort from the breathing process. Let energy and breath be all you are aware of. With no effort on your part, breathing will become smooth, with no jerkiness. It will become free from unnecessary noise and gradually it will become deeper and will measure itself in an even, harmonious rhythm. Allow your breathing to become an unbroken cycle in which inhalation becomes exhalation and vice versa without a break.

Now we will explore the subtle energy field of the body, co-ordinating mind, energy and body in the process.

Check you are in touch with the flow of air at the point where the bridge of the nose meets the upper lip. Follow the next inhalation up the nostrils and focus your awareness between the two eyebrows, allowing the face muscles to relax.

Now focus awareness on the larynx, at the pit of the throat.

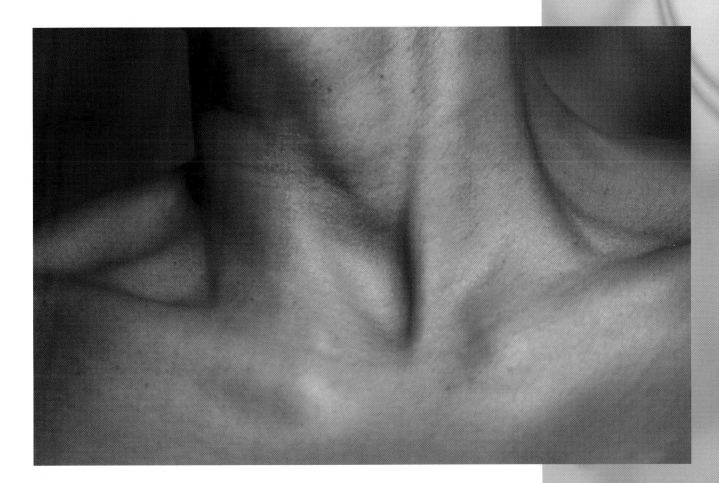

Follow the flow of energy through the left shoulder joint, down the upper arm to the elbow joint, feeling the energy in the forearm and its pulsing in the left wrist. Now follow its flow through to the tip of the thumb, index finger, middle finger, ring finger and little finger.

Follow the energy back through the left wrist, elbow, shoulder joint and rest awareness again in the larynx.

Repeat this sequence down the right side, shoulder, elbow, wrist, thumb and the four fingers and back again to the larynx.

Now follow the breath down to the "heart" centre, between the two breasts. From here, feel the flow of energy in the left breast, return to the heart, observe the energy in the right breast and again return to the heart centre.

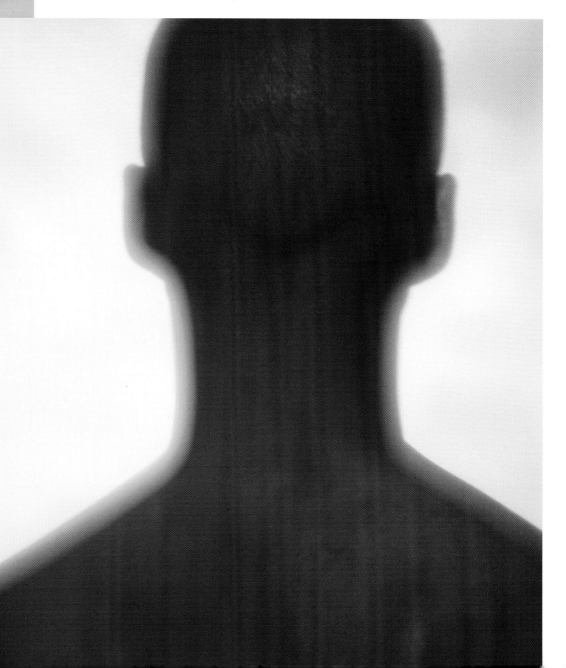

Behind the belly button is the solar plexus (knot of the sun) and behind that in the spine is the navel centre. Be in touch with the energy at this point and then sense the very base of the spine.

Now be aware of the energy flowing through the hip joint and down the left thigh to the knee. Then down to the left ankle and out through the toes, beginning with the big toe.

(Yes, it is possible to feel the energy in the toes!).Follow the flow of energy back through the left ankle, knee and hip joint to rest awareness again at the base of the spine.

Repeat this careful observation of the flow of energy for the right hip joint, knee, ankle, and the five toes and back to the base of the spine.

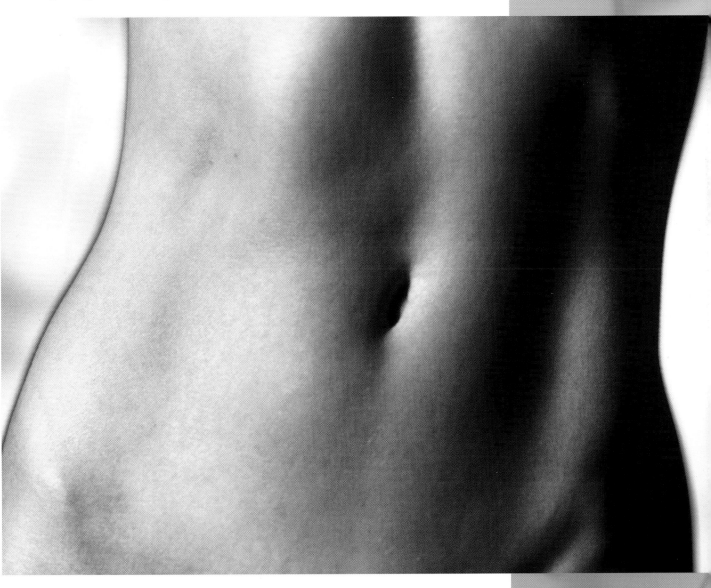

Now gradually focus the awareness of energy up the spine, through the navel centre, heart centre, larynx, the point between the two eyebrows and from here follow the breath down the nostrils again to be aware where the bridge of the nose meets the upper lip.

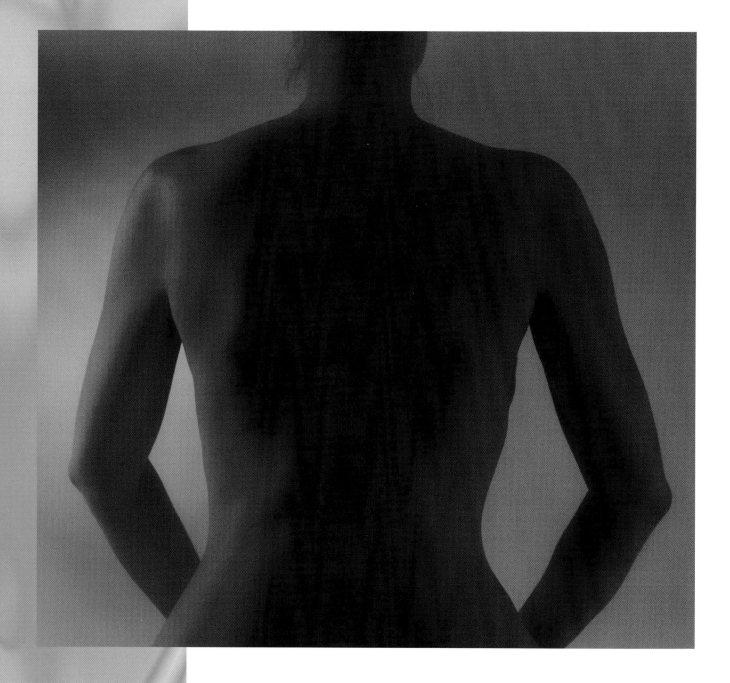

Below: take a moment to relax and delight in the vitality of the energy field which is both within you and all around you. Enjoy the feeling of its harmonious movement.

Take a moment to relax and delight in the vitality of the energy field which is both within you and all around you. Enjoy the feeling of its harmonious movement. Realise that the awareness that has enabled your steady observation of all these movements of energy is completely free of involvement with any of them.

Breath breathes. The expressions of life expand and contract. Awareness simply is.

This practice re-energises the energy system, co-ordinates body, breath and mind and is very therapeutic. Tension anywhere in the energy field is a cause of distress and eventually dis-ease. Intelligent, focused awareness is a great dissolver of tension. As the "knots" of tension dissolve, energy flows. Apart from these obvious benefits, the practice gradually restores the breath to its natural rhythm and depth, keeps you "in touch" and fosters meditative awareness.

Gradually all the activities of daily life will become more finely measured. Take a simple activity like opening and closing a door. Observe the quite unnecessary use of force often employed in this simple process. See the difference when the door is opened or closed with "in touch" awareness. In touch, all activities become more relaxed; combine this with the practice of falling still between activities already mentioned, and weariness and fatigue will become a thing of the past.

An ancient and authoritative text on meditative awareness, *Yoga Vasishtha*, states that the wise one, whatever the circumstances of life, remains aware of the movements in the mind.

A moment's reflection will show us that this is indeed a possibility and it points to an important fact. All that we encounter, whether they be physical objects in the material world or their more subtle counterparts seen in introversion or dreams, are witnessed in the mind through the light of awareness. We even, quite commonly, have conversations within ourselves, as though there was one person speaking a particular viewpoint and another listening and then responding with a different one. Consummate actors that we are, we all have a whole legion of personae which we more or less skillfully adopt according to the circumstances and company in which we find ourselves. All these masks of personality are, again, projected through the mind by the same light of awareness.

Above: all that we encounter are witnessed in the mind through the light of awareness.

Below: the light of awareness illuminates our experiences by day and our dreams by night – just as the sun constantly illuminates our universe.

Just as the sun that illumines our universe never sets, but only appears to do so because of the movements of the planet, so this light of awareness never sets within our being. It illuminates our experiences by day and our dreams by night. It remains constant even through our deepest sleep.

Even when the sun is obscured by clouds, it is still by its light that we can see the clouds. Similarly when the mind is burdened and "clouded over" by thoughts, it is the light of awareness that enables us to be aware of them. This light of awareness is what distinguishes the "quick" from the dead.

Consider this diagram:

BEING	BECOMING
Oject	Sense
Sound	Hearing
Feeling	Touching
From	Awareness
Seeing mind	Being
Flavour	Tasting
Scent	Smelling

This scheme of things is self-evident in our daily experience. It places mind as the central, transforming medium, like Newton's prism, through which our awareness of being is translated into the outward and visible signs of the objects of creation and, since it is a two-way process, these outward and visible signs are re-presented to our understanding. As the *Rig Veda* states (reproduced in the *Brihadaranyaka Upanishad*) in a hymn in praise of Indra, *The Pure Mind* (Hermes to the Greeks and Mercury to the Romans, in both cases messenger of the gods):

> *"That One Being was the matrix of every form — each of Its forms is for the purpose of self-recognition."*

Above: the first recorded words of Jesus Christ when he began to teach are given as "Repent, for the Kingdom of Heaven is at hand".

The first recorded words of Jesus Christ when he began to teach are given as "Repent, for the Kingdom of Heaven is at hand". Repenting has become confused with having remorse, but the root of the word indicates the resolution of the fivefold energies which make up our sensory experience back to their source.

This is confirmed by the original Greek text where the word used is *metanoia*, which literally means a complete turning of the mind so that the intelligence is established in its source, in Being, through meditative awareness, rather than being absorbed and involved in gross objects.

We can understand, and meditation enables us to realise, that the mind is like a two-way mirror. A mirror simply reflects what is presented to it. It does not discriminate and judge: "I don't like this face so I wont reflect it", or "I love this one so I will preserve it". It just reflects what is there. And since our lives are expressed through relationships at many levels, our relationship with our own bodies of experience, our families, friends and all the people we meet, with the environment, the ever-changing atmosphere, with the universe itself, the mind then fashions our response to what is reflected in our presence in such a way as to maintain harmony, efficiency and delight. Such is the ideal reflected in meditative awareness.

Above: meditation enables us to realise that the mind is like a two-way mirror.

Below: too often the mind is used not as a mirror but as a photographic plate, attempting to retain only the pleasant images reflected and avoiding that which caused discomfort or distress.

Unfortunately, too often the mind is used not as a mirror but as a photographic plate, attempting to retain only the pleasant images reflected and avoiding that which caused discomfort or distress. Soon the bright surface of the mind is covered by a confusion of prejudices, preconceptions, misconceptions, filled with certainties conceived through past experience which may well not be relevant to the present circumstance. The free flow of relationship is hindered by expectations and demands which are often quite unreasonable, as Shakespeare states: "Thus conscience doth make cowards of us all, and the native hue of resolution is sicklied o'er by the pale cast of thought."

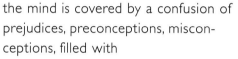

The answer to this, provided by meditative awareness, is to have respect, which means to look again. Just as we have come to realise the power of listening to sounds without putting a name to them or reacting with like or dislike of what we hear, so we can realise the value of just seeing without naming or reacting to what we see.

A group of students of meditation were invited to inspect a scallop shell, one of a pile provided as ashtrays in the meeting room. In a very short time the exercise was completed. It was an ashtray – so what? When invited to take another look, without naming, liking or disliking, the group took much longer in their inspection, with varying degrees of realisation of the harmony of the form, the delicacy and beauty of the colouring, the sheer "magic" of this superficially ordinary and everyday object.

I have also heard of a person roused from a daydream by the sight of a two-year-old contemplating a reproduction of the icon of the *Black Madonna* familiar from the Russian Orthodox tradition. Paying the same respectful attention to this image as the child, this person connected to the indissoluble bond of love between the mother of creation and her offspring – such is the sustaining power of meditative awareness.

*Right: to practise
meditative
awareness through
seeing we can
adapt a well-
known exercise
from yoga called
Trataka which
uses a candle
flame.*

To practise this meditative awareness through seeing we could use any visible object. We can also adapt a well-known exercise from yoga called Trataka which uses a candle flame. Light a candle and sit comfortably and at ease in a position where the candle can be watched without straining. Desire only to see the light of the flame. Now you are the seer and the flame is the object seen. Put another way, the light of awareness is connected to the light of the flame by the light energy of seeing. Maintaining this connection, you may realise that it is the same light which fulfills these three apparently different functions. Light, indeed, is one. Still maintaining this steady focus you may come to appreciate the clarity, beauty and intelligence of this relationship of light. See how the form harmoniously and efficiently reflects its function, then become aware that the clarity, beauty and intelligence is a reflection of yourself and delight in that awareness.

Angelus Silesius, a Christian mystic of the 17th century, wrote:

*"I myself the sun must be, shining clear and bright,
Painting life's lacklustre sea with God Itself as light."*

(from the Cherubinic Wanderer)

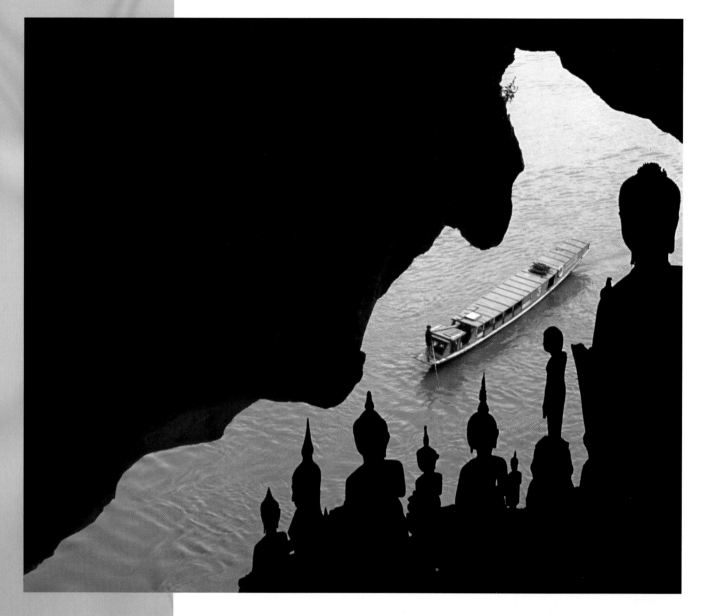

Socrates is reported to have said that "the unexamined life is not worth living". Here it seems reasonable to assume that he is not referring to a kind of post-mortem examination of our actions and responses, but a life lived without the benefit of the light of self-awareness. This is confirmed by his magnificent parable of the cave (*Republic*, Book 7) which he uses to show how far our nature is enlightened or unenlightened. Here, human beings have been trapped, since childhood, unable to see the light behind them and therefore only able to apprehend shadows thrown by this light onto the wall of the cave. This they take to be reality. This is much the case when we lose meditative awareness.

When, like the prisoners in Socrates' cave, we turn our backs on the meditative light of self-awareness we lose our natural harmony and co-ordination, along with our focus. It is not uncommon to be engaged in one activity in the physical world whilst our mind is elsewhere, daydreaming of other times and places. At the same time our emotional feelings are unconnected to either the mind or the body and not surprisingly our energies are all over the place. In short, we are out of touch. Natural contentment and joy are no longer obvious to us, so we are forced to seek fulfilment externally, expecting other people, events or objects to satisfy us. Self-delight and self-respect are lost to us – we seek them elsewhere.

This brings great instability to the mind which now embarks on a restless search for pleasure and satisfaction. Tension and anxiety become the norm as a result of this. Ideas, opinions and beliefs are taken to be true and the amassing of information is mistaken for knowledge. Significantly, much that passes for mass entertainment or amusement is designed to "take us out of ourselves", the implication being that "ourselves" is no longer a pleasant place to be.

Below: it is not uncommon to be engaged in one activity in the physical world whilst our mind is elsewhere, daydreaming of other times and places.

Natural composure and rest is lost, the mind becomes restless and filled with conflicting desires, even the composure of the body goes and we find it impossible to sit still in our own company for very long. Unsure of ourselves, we are barely able to have meaningful communication with others, let alone satisfying relationships. This gives rise, in varying degrees, to a general sense of discontent, dissatisfaction, unhappiness, despair and outright misery. Since our immune system seems, in a very real way, connected to our sense of well-being, it is not long before our health begins to suffer from this state of affairs. Illness is, after all, dis-ease.

We find ourselves apparently separate, weak and with very limited resources in what seems to be a hostile universe. Like the prodigal son in the parable, we have wasted our substance in riotous living and now have to feed on husks. Like the prodigal son we have to "come to ourselves" and return to the meditative light of self-awareness. For this we need meditation.

Above: daydreaming brings great instability to the mind which now embarks on a restless search for pleasure and satisfaction.

Far left: we find ourselves apparently separate, weak and with very limited resources in what seems to be a hostile universe.

Below: effective meditation will begin to reverse much of what has been described at the beginning of this chapter.

The means and methods of meditation are many and varied. Each individual must find for themselves that which is effective. Effective meditation will begin to reverse much of what has been described at the beginning of this chapter. Here are some indications of effective meditation.

SIGNS OF EFFECTIVE MEDITATION

An effective meditation technique gives rise to meditative awareness in the everyday concerns of life. This is almost axiomatic and hardly needs to be stated. The most clear and obvious manifestation of this is apparent in the personality and behaviour of the meditator – "By their fruits you will know them". A quiet, self-confident and very positive presence will be evident. With this will go a contentment which is not based on demands made on others. In fact, such a person will have time, space and capacity to attend to the needs of others, without making conditions or expecting rewards for this. Joy and contentment are inherent so there is no reliance on persons or objects for satisfaction. In this there is freedom to enjoy the moment without seeking to grasp or possess it.

Since meditation connects us to our centre and our source of Being, there will be an absence of self-criticism (in the negative sense) and no criticism of others.

Efficiency in worldly affairs without concern for the praise or blame of others would also be a mark of efficient meditation as would an integrity of speech and action. For example, to mean what one says and to act accordingly – to keep one's word.

Meditation gives rise to harmony of mind, energy and body. This is indicated by a sense of calm more or less free from excited elation or depression. There would be good physical health and rapid recovery in the case of illness. Freedom from fear and feelings of isolation and separation would result in the cessation of aggressive or selfish behaviour. Ultimately there would be no deliberate harm to others in thought, word or deed.

The joyful peace of meditative awareness extends to others unconditionally.

Above: effective meditation releases us from fear and feelings of isolation. Ultimately there would be no deliberate harm to others in thought, word or deed.

A SYSTEMATIC PRACTICE

Below: when preparing for systematic practice take the telephone off the hook and disconnect the doorbell to avoid any interruptions.

Here is a practice that will cultivate meditative awareness. It is an extension of the practice outlined in the chapter "Meditation through Breath". There it was suggested that you make your own recording on a cassette to guide yourself through the practice. This extension could be added to that recording, as appropriate.

Many have found that the regular practice of this exercise leads to a transformation of the conditions of their daily life – so do try it out.

To begin, make sure that you will not be disturbed. Take the telephone off the hook and disconnect the doorbell.

Now adopt the "corpse posture" familiar to students of yoga. Here you lie on your back, making sure your head, neck and spine are in a straight line. It may be good to support your head with a low pillow. The principle is that the body should be still, comfortable and relaxed. The arms should be slightly separate from the body, with the palms turned upwards and the legs should be spread apart.

The main criterion here is your own ease, so find a position in which you can be sure there will be no inconvenience or distraction.

Below: lie on your back, making sure your head, neck and spine are in a straight line.

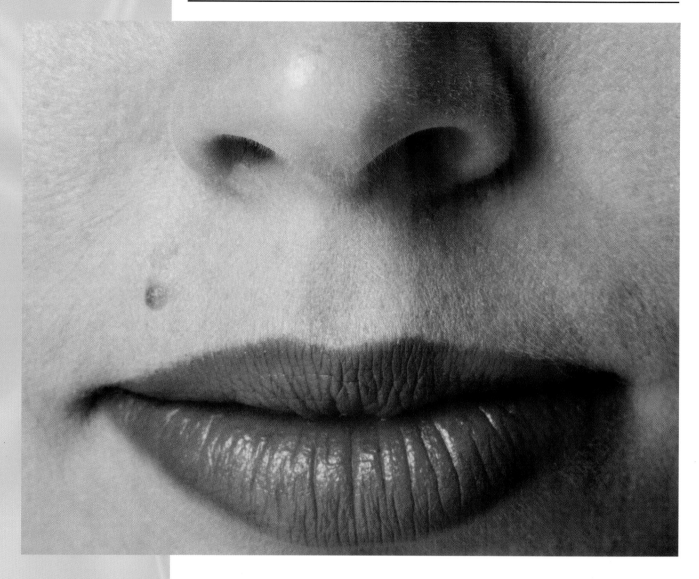

Above: focus your attention at the point where the bridge of the nose meets the upper lip.

Far right: move your awareness around the 61 energy points in the body.

Focus your attention at the point where the bridge of the nose meets the upper lip and be in touch with the feel of the air entering and leaving your body. Make sure that you are in touch. Intelligent observation at this point will reveal that the breath, with no effort on your part, becomes smooth, without any jerkiness. Extraneous noises in the breath will disappear, and, again without any contrivance on your part, the breathing will become even, so that exhalation and inhalation are the same. Now pay attention to the point where inhalation becomes exhalation, and vice versa. Without any interference on our part there is no pause or gap at this point. Naturally breathing is one unbroken cycle, encompassing these two functions of inhalation and exhalation. Simply observe this to be so.

Now move your awareness around the 61 energy points in the body as indicated earlier, co-ordinating mind with the flow of energy, getting in touch with the entire energy field of your body. Focusing again where the bridge of the nose meets the upper lip, concentrate on the energy field of the body from the crown of the head to the tips of the toes. Observe that, as you exhale, you are emptying yourself of all that is stale, all fatigue, stress and strain; as you inhale, the entire energy field is receiving life and vitality from the atmosphere around you. Exhale from the crown of the head right down to the tips of the toes and, as you inhale from the tips of the toes to the crown of the head, acknowledge the life, light and energy filling your energy field. Observe this for a few breaths.

Now we are gradually going to contract the field of awareness, so for a few breaths exhale from the crown of the head down to the ankles, and then inhale from the ankles to the crown of the head. Just be aware of the movements of energy between these two points.

Now exhale from the crown of the head down to the knee joints and inhale from the knee joints to the crown of the head, for a few breaths.

Right: exhale from the crown of the head down to the hip joints and inhale from the hip joints to the crown of the head for a few breaths

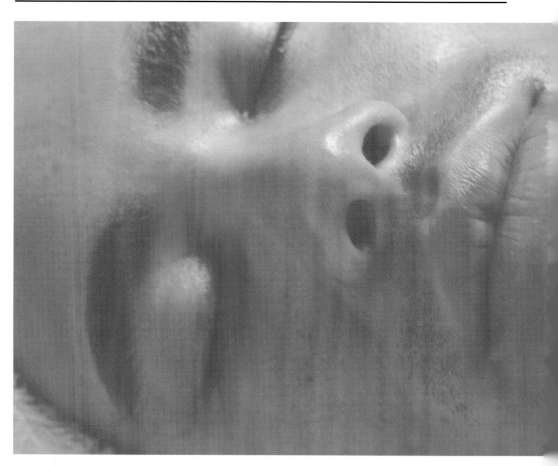

Exhale from the crown of the head down to the hip joints and inhale from the hip joints to the crown of the head for a few breaths

Exhale from the base of the spine to the crown of the head and inhale from the crown of the head back to the base of the spine for a few breaths. This simply means that the mind focuses only on the feeling of energy between these two points.

Now exhale from the navel centre, in the spine behind the belly button, behind the solar plexus, to the crown of the head and inhale from the crown of the head down to the navel centre for a few breaths.

Exhale from the heart centre to the crown of the head and inhale from the crown of the head down to the heart centre for a few breaths.

Now exhale from your throat centre, in the larynx, to the crown of the head and exhale from the crown of the head down to the throat centre for a few breaths.

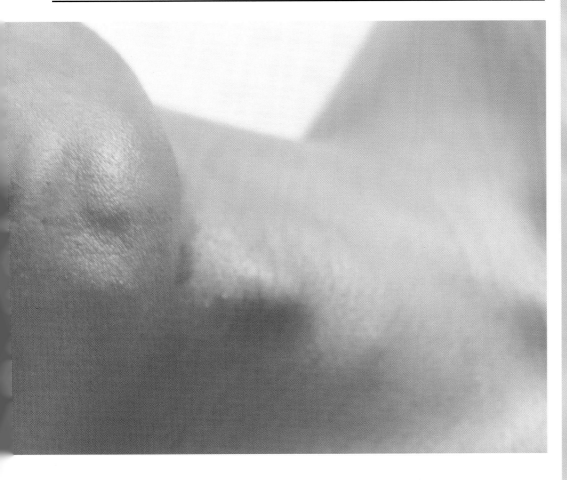

Exhale from the point where the bridge of the nose meets the upper lip to the crown of the head and inhale from the crown of the head to the point where the bridge of the nose meets the upper lip. Let your awareness focus only between these two points for a few breaths.

Now bring the focus of awareness to the space between the two eyebrows and the crown of the head. Observe the movements of energy in this space as you breathe in and out. Now the entire energy field of the body is at rest.

Systematically expand the field of awareness again. Inhale from the bridge of the nose to the crown of the head for a few breaths

Now focus on the energy field, in due order:

from the crown of the head down to the throat centre (larynx);

from the crown of the head down to the heart centre;

from the crown of the head down to the navel centre;

Above: this ancient mantra has been proven over the centuries – it can link the individual breath to the pattern of universal breath, bringing harmony to all the energy systems of the body.

from the crown of the head down to the base of the spine;

from the crown of the head down to the hip joints;
from the crown of the head down to the knee joints;

from the crown of the head down to the ankles.

Now be aware of the entire energy field of the body – without limits as to its extent. Observe the rhythmic, natural expansion and contraction of the energy field.

Now turn your awareness to sound and space. Simply desire to hear. Do not name the sounds you hear, just hear them as sound. Acknowledge how the sounds arise out of silence, reverberate through the silence and then dissolve back into silence. Focus your awareness on the silence.

Now, as you exhale, hear the sound SO carried on the breath and, as you inhale, hear the sound HUM. Let these sounds pervade the breath and fill the mind as you breathe. There is no effort required – just hear the mantra of the breath, So-Hum, So-Hum, So-Hum, So-Hum. This ancient mantra has been proven over the centuries – it can link the individual breath to the pattern of universal breath, bringing harmony to all the energy systems of the body.

Now you will be aware of the fact that all your experiences are illumined by one light of awareness. This light of awareness is entirely free of agitation. Like the silver screen of the cinema, it is totally unaffected by the objects it brings to light. Come fully to rest in this unagitated light of your own awareness.

Bathe in the light of Being. Now acknowledge the joy which is the very essence of your experience. Be in touch with this joy throughout the energy field of your body, then allow your awareness to flow out again to the sounds, sights and smells of your room and return to your daily business.

This practice, like all the others suggested in this text, is entirely natural, approved by a long tradition and harmless since it is within the capacity of each individual. It is designed to re-unite you with your birthright of meditative awareness

Below: even within these universally accepted guidelines there is an extensive range of practical advice from which we can choose.

RECOMMENDED READING

The methods and techniques which can be employed to bring us to meditation and self-awareness are, indeed, many and various. Since every human being is unique, some experimentation is required to find the path that most readily works for you. All systems agree on certain essentials: the ease and balance of the body; the co-ordination and harmony of the energy systems; the ability to focus the mind; and the need to discriminate between that which leads us towards joy and freedom and that which leads us astray. Even within these universally accepted guidelines there is an extensive range of practical advice from which we can choose. The list below is by no means exhaustive, but constitutes an impressive body of advice and instruction that should be of benefit to everybody.

THE POWER OF NOW
BY ECKHART TOLLE

A contempory teacher of non-dual
awareness speaks about the
establishment of self-awareness here
and now. His teaching in this book is
highly practical and couched in simple
terms.

THE BOOK OF SECRETS
BY OSHO

A series of explanatory discourses by
arguably one of the greatest masters
of meditation of the 20th century,
interspersed with questions and
answers from his audience of disciples.
The discourses are based on the
Vijnana Bhairava Tantra – an ancient
Sanskrit text which proposes 112
dharanas or methods of entering
meditation. Osho explains each one in
terms that make them readily available
to anybody interested enough to try
them out. Certainly at least one of
them will work for you.

THE SECRET OF SECRETS
BY OSHO

This series of discourses is based on
the *Secret of the Golden Flower*, an
ancient Chinese meditation text which
deals most scientifically with the
function of breath and vitality in the
process of self-realisation. This text is
particularly suitable for those who
naturally connect with the importance
of the breath in meditation.

THE OPEN SECRET
BY TONY PARSONS

A very accessible text by another
contemporary teacher who aims to
make meditative awareness, as his title
implies, available to all. Very user-friendly.

ESSENTIAL TAO
BY THOMAS CLEARY.

Tao is the great Chinese contribution
to the field of meditation and
meditative awareness. This book brings
us, in a fluent translation, Lao Tzu, Tao
Te Ching and the basic writings of
Chuang Tzu. Deeply thought-provoking
and full of good-humoured insight.

THE CLOUD OF UNKNOWING
THE EPISTLE OF PRIVY COUNCIL

Written by a monk in the 14th
century, this is the classic text on
Christian meditation. Written in a
robust and homely style, it will make
perfect sense and give great insight to
anybody seeking to meditate today.

YOGA SUTRAS OF PATANJALI

From the Vedic tradition, this is the
great authority on the science of yoga,
or union, in which meditation plays such
an important part. From your earliest
beginnings in the way of meditation,
right through to your fulfilment, this is a
reliable textbook and guide to the
understanding of everything that you
may encounter on your journey.

This is just a short selection from a vast library of texts which have been prepared throughout the ages to help those seeking any of the wonderful benefits of meditation. Once you start your sincere enquiry, you will be drawn towards that which will be most helpful to you. If I may, just before the end, I will add a few words of advice.

In this day and age we are all very much attuned to the written word. It carries its own authority in our society. The western Christian tradition flourished under a system of study known as: *Lectio* (reading), *Meditatio* (meditation) and *Oratio* (prayer).

This formula survived in the *Book of Common Prayer* in the phrase "Read, learn and inwardly digest."

To this day the written word is still paramount.

In the east, however, the oral tradition has always had an equal, if not greater, status as that which is written. The Vedic system of study also has three parts: *Sravanam* (hearing), *Mananam* (reflection) and *Nididhyasanam* (realisation).

This leads us to an important point to do with the discipline of reading. When reading anything, we should make sure that we can hear the sound of our own voice enunciating the text.

Naturally this is slower than the speed reading and scanning methods which have become quite popular today. These methods may well have their place if you have to deal quickly with large volumes of information, but generally do not lend themselves to inward digestion. How often, if you were asked what was it you just read, would you be able to answer accurately?

Reading is a wonderful gift – it gives us access to the wisdom of all ages and traditions. However, we should not fall into the trap of mistaking information for real knowledge. Particularly in respect of meditation, it is very rare for an individual to "progress" far without a teacher. When the desire is strong and the preparatory work has been done, no doubt you will find the appropriate guide to bring you to meditation. Meanwhile the good company of like-minded people can be a blessing. Although meditation itself is a totally singular affair, good company is a great source of strength, support and energy which may help us to transcend the limitations of our particular personalities.

Whatever your age, wherever your location, the desire for meditation and the sincere pursuit of this desire will surely light your way.

PATANJALIS EIGHTFOLD ELEMENTS

The science of Yoga (Union) has been comprehensively explained in this masterly text, which, though written down some two thousand years age, stands as the authority to this day in the Vedic Sanskrit philosophical tradition. It presents us with a systematic and holistic approach to meditative awareness which is presented in eight aspects.

The first of these is a series of five measures with which to regulate our relationships with others.

Of these the first, paradoxically, is said to be the culmination of the entire science. This is harmlessness, not to injure another in thought, word or deed. This is a very high ideal with practical applications at many levels. Patanjali gives a "litmus paper" test for a progress towards this. If harmlessness is perfected, aggression and violence cease in one's environment.

Then comes the practice of Truthfulness. The old Biblical injunction "Thou shalt not bear false witness" is a perfect statement of this measure. It is very much concerned with the trueness of our self expression. Again, there is an acid test. When truthfulness is perfected what we say will come to pass. The very basic requirement is that we keep our word-a sure sign of integrity of being.

Non-stealing is the next measure-not taking to ourselves what does not belong to us. Ultimately we are all burdened and possessed by our possessions and to some extent have all realized this in some way. As we free ourselves from this desire to take to ourselves beyond our true needs, to the same extent we become free to enjoy all the riches life has to offer.

Self-containment is prescribed next, a curb on the incessant wastage of energy, in all its many forms. Fidgeting and chattering are two obvious examples we could all work on with immediate good effect. As a result of self containment virility or creative energy would become increasingly available to us.

The last of this first series of measures is non-grasping. It is the ability to relax and let go. Meditative awareness is hidden from us if we have our nose in a mental "account book" full of debits and credits, obligations and requirements based on our past experiences.

The second element deals with another set of five measures more related to our inner awareness — our relationship within ourselves.

These begin with cleanliness, not only of the body but also of the mind and heart.

Then comes contentment, which really needs no commentary. A moments self reflection shows what a misery we create for ourselves through discontent – which is basically an inability to accept present reality!

A disciplined approach to life is next called for, which is very much a question of connection to natural measure, not to eat or sleep too little or too much are disciplines (or lack of) which we all face daily.

The fourth measure is to do with self examination, or self awareness, without which the final measure of being at all times true to oneself would not be possible.

These ten measures outlined in the first two elements of the system of Yoga are clearly all complimentary. Perfect one and the others would all fall into place. Clearly, only when we have begun to acknowledge them can meditative awareness begin to become available to us.

The third element is posture. Patanjali says that this should be steady and joyful. It arises through the total relaxation of effort. To the extent that effort is relaxed, our limitations begin to dissolve. All the different "postures" common to the practice of Hatha Yoga are designed to facilitate this total relaxation through which we may come to our still centre, at the same time developing strength of the physical body and refinement of the nervous system.

The fourth element deals with restoring the breath and the flow of vitality or the life force to its full measure. All the practices suggested in this book begin with connection to the breath and are entirely safe since they operate within your own comfortable capacity. Any other experimentation with breath should only be attempted under qualified supervision, such is the power of breath.

The fifth element is detachment. This is often translated as separating the senses from their objects. However this is not feasible since the senses and their objects are different aspects of the same energy and union will not be possible without their connection. What is required is that the witnessing, meditative awareness remains detached from the whole process of experiencing. This brings maximum freedom and full enjoyment-both.

Sixth, seventh and eighth elements describe the process of meditative awareness. The mind, in conjunction with the senses, focuses upon an object- this may be a sound, form, smell, feeling or indeed a taste. What begins as a gross-physical experience refines through ever expanding levels of awareness, until we stand alone fully established in meditative awareness.

All this is within reach of everyone of us ready to embark upon this fascinating and rewarding quest to " discover meditation"

INDEX

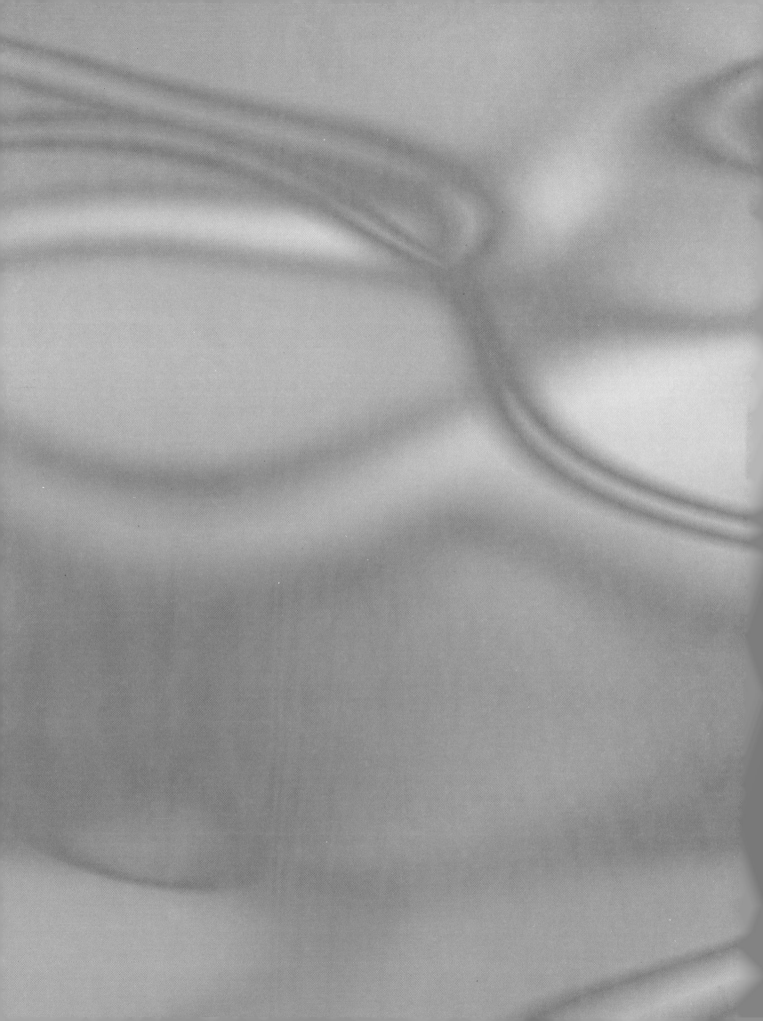